PROVERBS VOL.1

THE BEGINNING OF WISDOM

7 INTERACTIVE BIBLE STUDIES FOR SMALL GROUPS AND INDIVIDUALS

JOSHUA NG

matthiasmedia

PROVERBS VOL.1

The Beginning of Wisdom

Matthias Media
(St Matthias Press Ltd ACN 067 558 365)
PO Box 225
Kingsford NSW 2032
Australia
Telephone: (02) 9663 1478; international: +61-2-9663-1478
Facsimile: (02) 9663 3265; international: +61-2-9663-3265
Email: info@matthiasmedia.com.au
Internet: www.matthiasmedia.com.au

Matthias Media (USA)
Telephone: 330 953 1702; international: +1-330-953-1702
Facsimile: 330 953 1712; international: +1-330-953-1712
Email: sales@matthiasmedia.com
Internet: www.matthiasmedia.com

ISBN 978 1 921441 92 9

Cover design and typesetting by Lankshear Design Pty Ltd.

» CONTENTS

How to make the most of these studies 5

STUDY 1: The purpose of Proverbs 9

STUDY 2: Madam Folly and Lady Wisdom 15

STUDY 3: Wisdom from the world? 23

STUDY 4: The fear of the LORD 31

STUDY 5: Does Proverbs promise too much? 41

STUDY 6: Wisdom beyond Proverbs 47

STUDY 7: How to get wisdom 55

» HOW TO MAKE THE MOST OF THESE STUDIES

1. What is an Interactive Bible Study?

Interactive Bible Studies are a bit like a guided tour of a famous city. They take you through a particular part of the Bible, helping you to know where to start, pointing out things along the way, suggesting avenues for further exploration, and making sure that you know how to get home. Like any good tour, the real purpose is to allow you to go exploring for yourself—to dive in, have a good look around, and discover for yourself the riches that God's word has in store.

In other words, these studies aim to provide stimulation and input and point you in the right direction, while leaving you to do plenty of the exploration and discovery yourself.

We hope that these studies will stimulate lots of 'interaction'—interaction with the Bible, with the things we've written, with your own current thoughts and attitudes, with other people as you discuss them, and with God as you talk to him about it all.

2. The format

The studies contain five main components:

- sections of text that introduce, inform, summarize and challenge
- numbered questions that help you examine the passage and think through its meaning
- sidebars that provide extra bits of background or optional extra study ideas, especially regarding other relevant parts of the Bible
- 'Implications' sections that help you think about what this passage means for you and your life today
- suggestions for thanksgiving and prayer as you close.

3. How to use these studies on your own

- Before you begin, pray that God would open your eyes to what he is saying in the Bible, and give you the spiritual strength to do something about it.
- Work through the study, reading the text, answering the questions about the Bible passage, and exploring the sidebars as you have time.
- Resist the temptation to skip over the 'Implications' and 'Give thanks and pray' sections at the end. It is important that we not only hear and understand God's word, but respond to it. These closing sections help us do that.
- Take what opportunities you can to talk to others about what you've learnt.

4. How to use these studies in a small group

- Much of the above applies to group study as well. The studies are suitable for structured Bible study or cell groups, as well as for more informal pairs and triplets. Get together with a friend or friends and work through them at your own pace; use them as the basis for regular Bible study with your spouse. You don't need the formal structure of a 'group' to gain maximum benefit.

- For small groups, it is *very useful* if group members can work through the study themselves *before* the group meets. The group discussion can take place comfortably in an hour (depending on how sidetracked you get!) if all the members have done some work in advance.
- The role of the group leader is to direct the course of the discussion and to try to draw the threads together at the end. This will mean a little extra preparation—underlining the sections of text to emphasize and read out loud, working out which questions are worth concentrating on, and being sure of the main thrust of the study. Leaders will also probably want to work out approximately how long they'd like to spend on each part.
- If your group members usually don't work through the study in advance, it's extra important that the leader prepares which parts to concentrate on, and which parts to glide past more quickly. In particular, the leader will need to select which of the 'Implications' to focus on.
- We haven't included an 'answer guide' to the questions in the studies. This is a deliberate move. We want to give you a guided tour of the Bible, not a lecture. There is more than enough in the text we have written and the questions we have asked to point you in what we think is the right direction. The rest is up to you.

5. Bible translation

Previous studies in our Interactive Bible Study series have assumed that most readers would be using the New International Version of the Bible. However, since the release of the English Standard Version in 2001, many have switched to the ESV for study purposes. For this reason, we have decided to quote from and refer to the ESV text, which we recommend.

» STUDY 1

THE PURPOSE OF PROVERBS

1. Proverbs is a favourite part of the Bible for many Christians. We love its short, pithy insights into the nature of life in God's world, and its practical encouragements to live God's way. Share one or two of your favourite proverbs from Proverbs.
   - Why do you like them?
   - How do they help you in your Christian life?

MOST OF THE INDIVIDUAL sayings in Proverbs are very short. Some run for several verses but most are just a single verse, and seemingly stand on their own. And this is how we tend to think of Proverbs—as a fairly random collection of little snippets of wisdom, each of which can be understood and applied fairly easily to our lives.

However, understanding the book of **Proverbs as a whole** takes a bit more time and effort. As with any part of the Bible, knowing the whole context enables us to apply any individual portion of God's word properly, so that we see and feel more sharply the challenge of its encouragements and rebukes. And Proverbs is no exception. Let us begin this series of studies by looking at the purpose of Proverbs.

Proverbs as a whole

Our favourite Proverbs most likely come from chapters 10-31 of Proverbs. This main section consists of six collections of proverbial sayings, each headed by the phrase, "The proverbs/words/ sayings of ...":

i. "The proverbs of Solomon." (10:1)
ii. "Incline your ear, and hear the words of the wise ..." (22:17)
iii. "These also are sayings of the wise." (24:23)
iv. "These also are proverbs of Solomon which the men of Hezekiah king of Judah copied." (25:1)
v. "The words of Agur son of Jakeh. The oracle." (30:1)
vi. "The words of King Lemuel. An oracle that his mother taught him ..." (31:1)

Read any verses at random from Proverbs 1-9.

2. How are these chapters different in style from chapters 10-31?

3. Now glance quickly over Proverbs 1-9, and try to summarize the emphasis of these chapters in a sentence or two.

4. Look up the following verses from Proverbs 1-9 (if you are studying in a group, you might like to divide them up among group members). In each case, who is talking to whom? And what kind of 'talk' is it?

- 1:8
- 2:1
- 3:1
- 3:11-12
- 4:1
- 4:10-11
- 4:20
- 5:1-2
- 6:1-3
- 6:20-22
- 7:1-3
- 7:24
- 8:32-34

5. Based on what you've looked at so far, how would you say Proverbs 1-9 relates to Proverbs 10-31?

While some speak of Proverbs 1-9 as the first collection of proverbs, it is more like an introduction or preparation for the six collections of sayings that follow. It is not so much a 'pep talk' as a '*prep* talk', as when a father says, "Come on, son, let's sit down and talk man to man, and I'll teach you what life is all about".

Proverbs assumes that teaching and wisdom ought to flow from parent to child. Moreover, the father is seen as none other than Solomon himself (1:1), the great wise man of the Old Testament. Proverbs 1-9 thus functions as an introductory framework through which we are to read chapters 10-31.

To see exactly how Proverbs 1-9 introduces and frames chapters 10-31, let's first look at Proverbs 1:1-7, which is like the 'introduction to the introduction'.

Read Proverbs 1:1-7.

6. What are the explicitly stated purposes of this book that is known as "The proverbs of Solomon"?

7. Who is it for?

8. How do we get this wisdom?

It is important to notice first that in outlining the purposes of Proverbs, this **'introduction to the introduction'** begins to tell us what 'wisdom' really is.

Wisdom involves knowledge—it includes knowing instruction and understanding words of insight (1:2). We need to put our minds into gear. Yet it is not merely theoretical, but immensely practical for daily living. Thus it's about "wise dealing", "prudence", and showing "discretion" in what we do and say (1:2-4). In other words, the wise person carefully weighs things up, rather than just acting on impulse and then regretting the consequences. Yes, wisdom involves learning, but it is learning that gives guidance for life (1:5). It's not about getting a master's degree, so much as mastering life. Wisdom is about being 'street smart', rather than just having lots of theoretical knowledge. It's the difference between someone who just graduated with an MBA, and someone who has been out there in the business world for ten years and knows how to deal with people and achieve successful outcomes. As Derek Kidner puts it: "Wisdom leaves its signature on anything well made or well judged ... an apt remark ... a shrewd policy ... noble action".[1]

Proverbs would say that what's important is not your IQ, but your WQ—your 'wisdom quotient'!

Wisdom, then, is for all people. If we are the "simple" who foolishly love being simple (1:22), then we really need to repent and so gain prudence (1:4). If we are already the "wise", then let us not think we have arrived, but know that we need more wisdom and can "increase in learning" (1:5). Unlike our IQ, our WQ can keep increasing, no matter who we are.

Introduction to the introduction

The climax of this 'introduction to the introduction' tells us that the key to the getting of wisdom is "the fear of the LORD" (1:7). We will come back to this in much more detail in study 4.

Furthermore, Proverbs 1:6 indicates that one purpose of Proverbs as a whole is that we may be able to understand any particular proverb, the way it expresses itself, as well as its meaning and application. No single proverb ultimately stands on its own, or says everything there is to say about a topic. That is, we must understand the part in the light of the whole. To rightly understand and apply any individual proverbial saying, we need not only the framework of Proverbs 1-9, but also the content and context of the rest of the book of Proverbs. But more of that in study 7.

» Implications

- In what areas of life do you think you need guidance to increase your WQ?

- "To obey the Bible is to be the truly practical person." Comment. Is this always true?

- Look back at the favourite proverbs you mentioned at the beginning of this study. How do they fit into the overall purpose of Proverbs?

» Give thanks and pray

- Thank God that he cares for us and wants to instruct us in practical living.
- Given the purpose of Proverbs, write a prayer for yourself as you embark on this series of studies.

Endnote

1. D Kidner, *Proverbs: An introduction and commentary*, Tyndale Old Testament Commentaries, DJ Wiseman (gen. ed.), IVP, Leicester, 1964, p. 13.

» STUDY 2

MADAM FOLLY AND LADY WISDOM

HAVING LOOKED AT THE PURPOSE of Proverbs outlined explicitly in Proverbs 1:1-7, let's now turn our attention to the series of fatherly talks in Proverbs 1:8-9:18, and see how they unpack further what it means to be wise ... and foolish! It can be summarized as the choice between 'two paths' and 'two women'.

Two paths

1. Read through as many of the passages in the following table as possible, and jot down brief observations under the following headings. What is the character of folly and wisdom? And what is the outcome of each path? (Note: not every passage has something for every heading. And try not to get bogged down in details. If you are working in a group, divide the passages up among members of the group.)

	Folly		Wisdom	
Proverbs	Character	Outcome	Character	Outcome
1:8-19	Following violent men, abusing the innocent for unjust gain	Backfiring on themselves, life taken away	Like a graceful garland on head	

Proverbs	Folly		Wisdom	
	Character	Outcome	Character	Outcome
1:20-33	Hating knowledge not listening to wisdom's reproof, complacent	Disaster and death, laughed at by wisdom	Desiring us to heed her correction	Dwelling secure
2:1-22				
3:1-35				
4:1-27				
5:1-23				
6:1-19				
6:20-8:36				

2. In the light of the above passages and table:

- Is there anything that surprises you about either folly or wisdom?

- Why is folly so enticing, and how is its attractiveness a lie?

- Summarize in your own words the benefits of wisdom.

- What do you think is the overall logic of the father's argument?

- How do you feel this 'prep talk' has motivated you to follow wisdom and avoid folly?

THE FATHER'S ARGUMENT IS BASICALLY 'Two ways to live', or more precisely, 'One way to live and one way to die'. The metaphor of the two paths begins with the greedy ambushers in 1:11 who call out, "Come with us". Solomon warns his son, "do not walk in the way with them; hold back your foot from their paths" (1:15). Wisdom herself cries out in the streets to warn the "simple ones" not to follow the wrong path and be destroyed, but to follow the way of wisdom and to dwell secure (1:33).

The metaphor is as simple as it is powerful. It involves walking (living), along a certain path (either the pattern of evil or of righteousness), heading in a certain direction towards a certain destination (either life or death). At the climax of this metaphor the father encourages his son to "ponder the path of your feet; then all your ways will be sure. Do not swerve to the right or to the left; turn your foot away from evil" (4:26-27). In other words, "Don't be stupid. Be sensible and choose life!"

Here then is what it means to be wise and to be foolish. To be wise is to act and live in such a way that will result in a good outcome. To be foolish is to act and live in such a way that will result in a bad outcome. This 'cause and effect' paradigm is a constant feature of Proverbs.

While this metaphor of 'two paths' permeates chapters 1-9, it is gradually subsumed under the theme of the 'two women'. First, there is the seductive adulteress (2:16-19 and chapters 5-7). Then there is the very personification of wisdom, Lady Wisdom herself (1:20-33 and 8:1-31). Their rivalry comes to a head in Proverbs 9.

Two women

Read Proverbs 9:1-6 and 9:13-18.

3. What is similar in the way these two women are presented? How does this highlight their rivalry?

4. What are the key differences between them? How do they remind you of the two women described in the earlier chapters?

5. On the surface, the contrast between the two women throughout these chapters seems mainly to be about adultery. Do you think it is about more than physical adultery? If so, why? If not, why not?

(Remember, Proverbs is cast as a father warning his son, and hence the temptress is female. Daughters need to be just as wary of the Casanovas of this world.)

Sex without responsibility—'casual sex'—is seen as normal and desirable in our society. The fact that it's a bit 'naughty' and has to be done in secret makes it all the more pleasurable and exciting. But just as the highway robbers' promise of 'easy money' is the path of folly (in chapter 1), so the adulteress's offer of 'easy sex' epitomizes the overall seduction of folly itself. The woman named 'Folly' stands for the life of foolishness as a whole (9:13). To embrace her is exciting. She promises pleasure: "Come, let us take our fill of love till morning; let us delight ourselves with love" (7:18). She promises secrecy: "For my husband is not at home; he has gone on a long journey" (7:19). All folly, says Proverbs, is persuasive like that.

Yet the pleasure does not last: "none who touches her will go unpunished" (6:29). You will be found out, and the jealous fury of her husband cannot be pacified (6:32-35). Many a man has suffered "wounds and disgrace" at the hands of a rightly jealous husband.

The closing verses of chapter 9 summarize the situation by saying in effect: "You want to end up in the company of the dead? Then go right ahead." Adultery is exciting, but stupid. To embrace a life of folly is no different.

By contrast, the life of wisdom in Proverbs is personified as Lady Wisdom. She calls on the stupid to turn to her by leaving their simple ways (9:1-6). She draws a contrast between the scoffer, who scorns the opportunity to learn by abusing the one who rebukes him, and the wise man, who loves to be rebuked for he sees it as an opportunity to grow wiser still. She urges the simple to come to her for life: "For *by me* your days will be multiplied, and years will be added to your life" (9:11). It's your own future that is at stake. If you know what's good for you, follow Lady Wisdom.

Lady Wisdom and Madam Folly thus represent two contradictory world views, with opposing lifestyles to match. The stakes are high, resulting in either life or death. Which woman are we going to follow? Proverbs 9 brings us climactically to this choice that we all must make. This is the choice that colours how we respond to all the individual proverbial sayings in chapters 10-31.

Lady Wisdom

Lady Wisdom not only appears as the climax to chapters 1-9 of Proverbs; we also catch a glimpse of her again in the final chapter of Proverbs—the famous picture of the "excellent wife" in Proverbs 31. This supremely upright and noble woman, who understands and lives out all the wisdom that Proverbs teaches, is an embodiment of Lady Wisdom. While this may not ease the pressure on wives to follow her example (she still is a literal woman whom wives should emulate), it does motivate all of us to embrace the life that Lady Wisdom offers.

» Implications

- Many of us have a three-tiered way of categorizing the choices we make in the Christian life:
  Tier 1: Right/wrong decisions
  Tier 2: Wise/foolish decisions
  Tier 3: Decisions about matters of indifference
  - A Christian sister says to you, "It's okay for me to keep going out with this non-Christian guy, isn't it? I mean, I know it's not wise, but it's not sinful is it?" How would you respond?
  - What impact does our study of Proverbs 1-9 so far have on this three-tiered system? (Also see, for example, 1:3, 2:9-22.) What are some implications of this? (You might also consider Mark 7:20-22—notice the surprising characteristic that is listed at the end of this list of sins.)

- Are there any ways in which you are flirting with Madam Folly? Do you think what you're doing is as stupid as committing adultery?

- Just how good do you think following Lady Wisdom really is? Share how it has manifested in your own life.

» Give thanks and pray

- Give thanks to God that he wants us to have 'the good life', and in his kindness, he warns us of and dissuades us from the dangers of folly.
- Speak to God about the ways in which you are tempted to follow foolishness, and ask him to show and lead you in the way of wisdom through the book of Proverbs.

» STUDY 3

WISDOM FROM THE WORLD?

1. "What's the key to getting wise?" What varied responses would people from different cultures give to this question?

Would they be varied or would they be much the same worldwide and adapted to lifestyle & circumstances.

DIFFERENT CULTURES HAVE THEIR different paths to wisdom. For some, it is listening to the latest internationally acclaimed speaker on 'How to be successful'. For others, it is listening to their mothers. Some rely on their own life experience; others on getting ahead in formal education as quickly as possible. Moreover, all cultures have their own proverbs and aphorisms, from ancient Confucius to the latest bumper sticker. What's more, some of these sources of wisdom seem to satisfy our definition of 'wisdom' (from study 2)—that is, they result in a good outcome.

So does Proverbs (or the Bible in general) have a monopoly on wisdom? Or can Christians get wisdom from the secular world? Isn't worldly wisdom … well, worldly? How much can we trust it?

Proverbs and ancient wisdom

It is possible that parts of Proverbs itself are actually collections of wisdom sayings from the pagan world. Thus Proverbs 30 is from Agur, son of Jakeh; and Proverbs 31:1-9 from King Lemuel (or indeed his mother!). As far as we know, neither of these men was an Israelite.

Furthermore, there are close parallels between Proverbs 22:17-24:22 and *The Instructions of Amenemope*, which is an Egyptian piece of proverbial literature written before the time of Solomon.

2. Read the following wise sayings from *The Instructions of Amenemope*, and compare each with the corresponding sayings from Proverbs.

The Instructions of Amenemope (30 chapters)	**Proverbs**
Give your ears and hear what is said, Give your mind over to their interpretation: It is profitable to put them in your heart ... (from chapter 1)	Incline your ear, and hear the words of the wise, and apply your heart to my knowledge, for it will be pleasant if you keep them within you, if all of them are ready on your lips. That your trust may be in the LORD, I have made them known to you today, even to you. (Prov 22:17-19)
Mark for your self these 30 chapters: They please, they instruct, They are the foremost of all books; They teach the ignorant. (from chapter 30)	Have I not written for you thirty sayings of counsel and knowledge ... (Prov 22:20)
Beware of stealing from a miserable man And of raging against a cripple. Do not stretch out your hand to touch an old man, Nor snip at the words of an elder. (from chapter 2)	Do not rob the poor, because he is poor, or crush the afflicted at the gate, for the LORD will plead their cause and rob of life those who rob them. (Prov 22:22-23)
Do not displace the surveyor's marker on the boundaries of the arable land, Nor alter the position of the measuring line; Do not be greedy for a plot of land ... (from chapter 6)	Do not move an ancient landmark or enter the fields of the fatherless, for their Redeemer is strong; he will plead their cause against you. (Prov 23:10-11)

Do not fraternize with the hot-tempered man, Nor approach him to converse. (from chapter 9)	Make no friendship with a man given to anger, nor go with a wrathful man ... (Prov 22:24)
Do not covet the property of the dependant Nor hunger for his bread; The property of the dependant blocks the throat, It is vomit for the gullet. Do not eat a meal in the presence of a magistrate, Nor set to speaking first. If you are satisfied with false words, Enjoy yourself with your spittle. (from chapters 11 and 23)	Do not eat the bread of a man who is stingy; do not desire his delicacies, for he is like one who is inwardly calculating. "Eat and drink!" he says to you, but his heart is not with you. You will vomit up the morsels that you have eaten, and waste your pleasant words. (Prov 23:6-8)
As to a scribe who is experienced in his position, He will find himself worthy of being a courtier. (from chapter 30)	Do you see a man skillful in his work? He will stand before kings; he will not stand before obscure men. (Prov 22:29)

- What similarities can you see between *The Instructions of Amenemope* and the references in Proverbs?

Which were written first?
Different cultures proverbs are known to others & adapted and adapted.
The Spanish proverb "There are no pockets in a shroud" is known in Scotland as "There's nae pooches in a shroud" but has the same meaning of "You can't take it with you."

- If the author of this part of Proverbs has adopted wisdom sayings from a pagan nation like Egypt, why do you think he has done so?

He lebet home!

- Look back over the table on pages 24-25. What *differences* do you notice between Proverbs and Amenemope?

Few)

Observation and experience of the world

Optional question: Can you think of some proverbial sayings from your culture that are derived from observation of the world? (E.g. 'A stitch in time saves nine'.)

Do people need to know the true God before they can get wisdom that's true? In one sense, we could say obviously not, for even ancient pagan Egypt had proverbial sayings that taught very similar wisdom to Proverbs.

But the principle is broader than that. It seems quite possible to gain wisdom simply from **observation and experience of the world.** Thus the famed Proverbs 6:6-8 can call upon the lazy sluggard to consider the natural diligence of the ant, and get wise! We might illustrate this way of gaining wisdom like this:

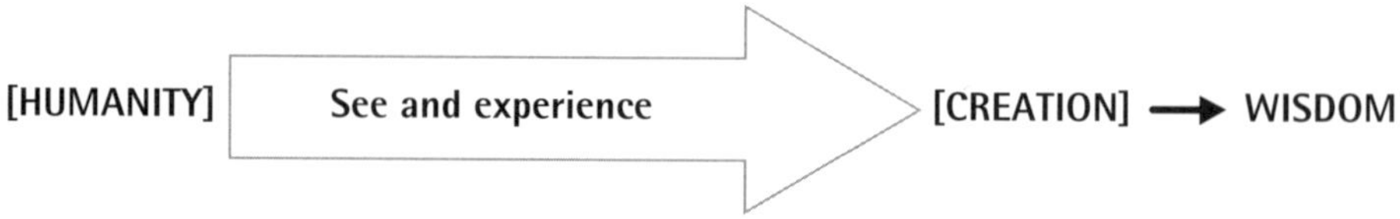

However, what is distinctive about Proverbs 22:17-24:22 is that it keeps bringing God into the picture. From the very outset, the reason for heeding these "thirty sayings of the wise" is so that you may trust in the LORD (Prov 22:17-19). And the section closes with the call to "fear the LORD" (Prov 24:21-22).

Ultimately, wisdom comes from God. But what is the connection between 'wisdom', 'creation', 'God' and 'humanity'?

God's wisdom and creation

Read Proverbs 8:22-31.

3. Who is the speaker? (See Proverbs 8:12.)

Modern knowledge would say Jesus

4. Why, then, can anybody look at the ant (6:6) and get wisdom?

Is it wisdom? What about a simple lesson that the ants and bees work for the continuation of the species. The lazy human if all were the same would end the species. Extinction by idleness.

5. Let's modify our diagram a little by adding a lens through which we view the world.[1] From our study so far, what is the lens that helps us see creation more clearly to gain wisdom?

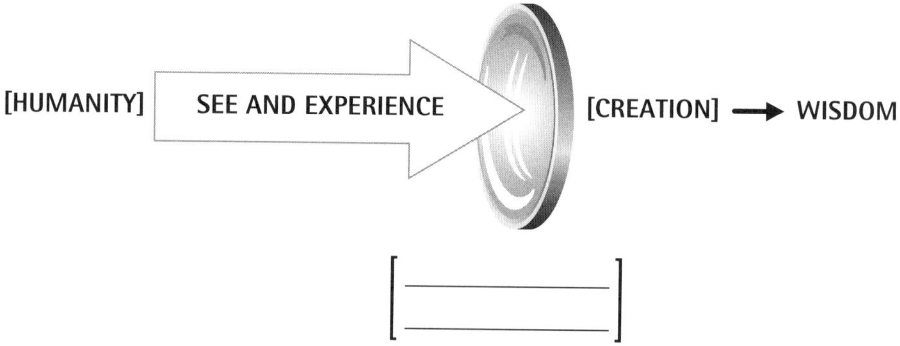

THROUGH HIS WISDOM, GOD HAS created things to function in a certain way. There is rhyme and reason, and purpose and order to this world. God's wisdom is 'hardwired' into the world he has made. That's why we can generally expect certain actions to have good consequences, and others bad consequences. That is also why even pagans who do not know God can gain wisdom from their experience of the world. The ancient Egyptian wisdom of Amenemope is just one of many examples of this in human cultures throughout history.

Nevertheless, once we hear such wisdom in Proverbs—that is, through God's Scriptural revelation itself—we see with far more *clarity* and *certainty* what we are meant to learn from his creation.

6. How then might you improve on the diagram on page 28?

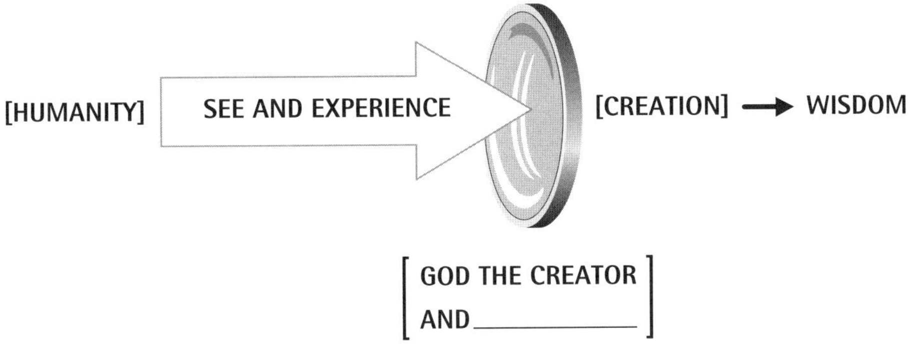

You would need to understand it in the first place.

» Implications

- Besides learning diligence from the famous ant (Prov 6:6-11), we can also learn from the hunted gazelle and the trapped bird (Prov 6:1-5). Can you think of other aspects of creation from which we can learn wisdom?

- Give examples of wisdom from the general non-Christian world that are quite sensible and wise (e.g. 'Money doesn't bring happiness').

- Are there any biblical backings for such wisdom that will give us greater confidence to follow such 'worldly wisdom'?

» Give thanks and pray

- Thank God for the orderly creation he has made through his wisdom, such that we can learn from creation, and expect wise actions to have good consequences and foolish actions to have bad consequences.
- Pray that we will keep on reading the Bible, God's clearest and most authoritative word, so that we can rightly assess and put creation's and the world's wisdom into perspective.

Endnote

1. Bruce Waltke also uses a similar analogy of a lens through which the people viewed creation to gain wisdom in his commentary, *The Book of Proverbs Chapters 1-15* (The New International Commentary on the Old Testament, RK Harrison and Robert L Hubbard, Jr. [gen. eds], Eerdmans, Grand Rapids, 2004), p. 55.

» STUDY 4

THE FEAR OF THE LORD

As we saw in our last study, one of the things that made Proverbs quite different from Amenemope was that Proverbs kept talking about "the fear of the LORD". Indeed, this takes us back to the very beginning of the book, to the climax of the 'introduction to the introduction', where the writer asserts, "The fear of the LORD is the beginning of knowledge; fools despise wisdom and instruction" (Prov 1:7).

But what does it mean to *fear* the LORD?

1. What do you think it means to fear someone?

Fear

2. Look up the following references from Proverbs 1-9, and fill in the table. (Not every reference will apply to both columns.)

Proverbs	What does it mean to fear the LORD?	Who is the LORD? What is he like?
1:7		
1:29-30		
2:5-7		
3:5-8		
3:9-12		
3:25-26		
3:31-32		
5:20-21		
6:16-19		
8:13		
8:35-36		
9:10		

- Can you see any link between who the LORD is and what it means to fear him?

- Is there any sense in which we need to be *afraid* of the LORD? Why/why not?

Who is the Lord? He is the creator and source of wisdom. He sees all we do and assesses our actions. He hates sin and punishes the wicked. He loves and approves of godliness, and protects the wise. The Lord lovingly disciplines us as a father would his son.

To fear *this* Lord thus involves knowing and trusting him, since he knows what's best for us. It means not being wise in our own eyes, as Eve was when she ate the forbidden fruit. It involves hating the sin that the Lord hates, and seeking to bring a smile to his face in all that we do. To fear him is to forgo pride, and instead to accept his loving reproof.

While 'reverence' and 'awe' are often used to describe our attitude of *fearing* the Lord, it blunts the sharp edge of the word 'fear'. It is quite right to be afraid of the Lord. Be very afraid! For if we reject him and follow folly, the resulting bad consequences come not as some automatic impersonal, mechanistic 'karma', but at the hand of this personal God.

The Lord

Moreover, this personal God has a personal name: 'the Lord', or literally **YHWH** in the Hebrew Scriptures.

Read Exodus 3:13-17 and 6:1-8.

3. Why do you think God revealed his name to Moses and the Israelites at this particular time in their history?

YHWH

In Hebrew, the name of God consists of four letters equivalent to the English letters YHWH. However, the Jews have always regarded the name of God as so holy that it should not be pronounced. (That's why we don't really know how it should be pronounced; 'YaHWeH' is our best guess.) Instead of pronouncing the name, the Jews would say "Adonai"—which means 'Lord'—whenever they came across YHWH in the Scriptures. Our English translations have followed this tradition by printing "Lord" (in small capitals) whenever God's personal name YHWH appears in the original text.

4. What significance would God's name have had for Israel in the generations to come?

It is often suggested that the book of Proverbs is really a general book of wisdom based only on creation, without any real connection to the story of Israel. And it is certainly true that Proverbs often bases its wisdom on God's creation of the world.

But the God who keeps being referred to in Proverbs is not a general creator God but YHWH, the personal God whom Israel experienced as he redeemed her from slavery in Egypt and bound himself to her by covenant.

Thus while many individual proverbial sayings may seem timeless and written for all humans everywhere, the right way to interpret them is through the fear of the Lord, who not only created Israel but saved her. As Proverbs 23:11 explicitly asserts, he is none other than her "Redeemer".

In fact, there are many more links to **God's salvation of Israel in Proverbs** than the book is usually given credit for. Most noticeably, the majority of the sayings and indeed the book as a whole are attributed to King Solomon, who ruled Israel at the height of the kingdom (cf. 1 Kings 1-10). Moreover, there are many incidental references to life in Israel.

God's salvation of Israel in Proverbs

Proverbs assumes that the wise life will be lived in the Promised Land into which YHWH has delivered Israel. Instructions about this land of their inheritance include not moving an ancient boundary stone set up by their forefathers (Prov 22:28, 23:10-11; cf. Deut 19:14, 27:17). There are many references to the Law itself (Prov 28:4, 7, 9; 29:18). The uncanny overlap between the moral instructions of Proverbs and those of the Mosaic Law in Exodus, ▶

On the flip side, the Law of Moses is spoken of in terms of wisdom (Deut 4:6-8; Ps 19:7). Obedience to the Mosaic Law was to be motivated not by an impersonal legalism but by the fear of the LORD, as in Proverbs (e.g. Deut 6:1-2). Indeed, the theme of wisdom versus folly is sprinkled throughout the history of Israel's salvation: from Joseph's wisdom as Pharaoh's second-in-command, to Moses' triumph over the 'wise' Egyptian magicians, to the prophecy of Isaiah and Jeremiah, to Daniel's wisdom in interpreting dreams in Babylon.

So there is not quite so much of a gulf between Proverbs and Israel's history as we might be led to believe. What this means for us practically is that we are to read Proverbs as first and foremost wisdom *for God's saved people*, rather than simply general wisdom for humanity. Proverbs shows how God's people are to live in God's Promised Land under his kingship. It is the fear of *this* LORD, not just any creator God, that is the beginning of wisdom (Prov 9:10).

Here's where we got to with our wisdom diagram at the end of study 3:

Leviticus and Deuteronomy should therefore come as no surprise. These include not only 'ethical' instructions —for example, concerning adultery (Prov 5-7; Exod 20:14) and unjust scales (Prov 20:23; Lev 19:36)— but also 'ceremonial' laws to honour the LORD with the first fruits from the land (Prov 3:9; Deut 26).

Moreover, the sacrificial law of Leviticus is assumed, for "to do righteousness and justice is more acceptable to the LORD than sacrifice" (Prov 21:3; cf. 1 Sam 15:22; see also Prov 15:8, 21:27). Indeed, to reject the Law is foolish, for it brings about the ejection from *the land* (Prov 2:21-22, 10:30), echoing Moses' famous covenant warnings in Deuteronomy 28.

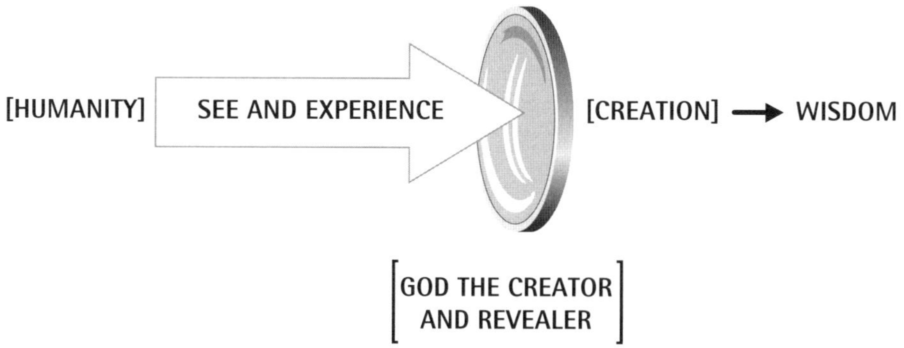

5. In light of what we've seen so far in this study, how might we fine-tune the diagram even more?

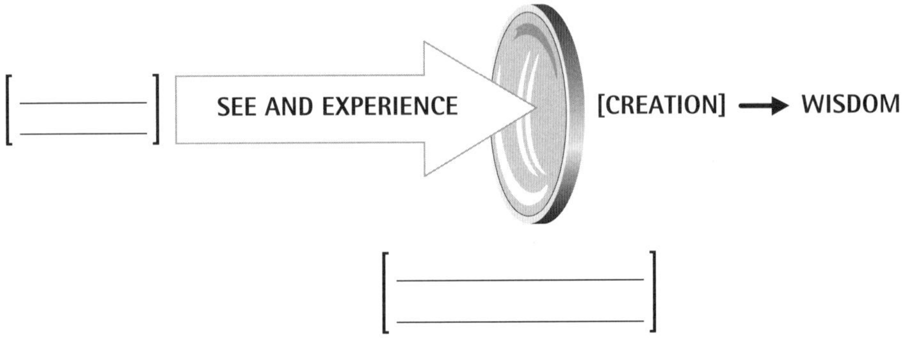

The beginning of wisdom

"THE FEAR OF THE LORD IS THE beginning of knowledge; fools despise wisdom and instruction" (Prov 1:7).

The title of this first volume of our studies in Proverbs is *The Beginning of Wisdom*. So far in this study we have looked at both who this LORD is and what it means to fear him. But in what sense is the fear of the LORD the *beginning* of wisdom?

Read (on the one hand) Proverbs 1:7 and 9:10, and (on the other) Proverbs 2:1-15.

6. What is the relationship between 'getting wisdom' and 'the fear of the LORD'? See if you can draw a diagram to represent it.

7. Do you think the following quotes capture what Proverbs means by the 'beginning' of wisdom? Why/why not? Which one do you think is better?

- "What the alphabet is to reading, notes to reading music, and numerals to mathematics, the fear of the LORD is to attaining the revealed knowledge of this book."[1]
- "Just as the rotating observation deck at the top of Centrepoint Tower is a great vantage point from which to see the whole city of Sydney, so is the 'fear of the LORD' when it comes to viewing wisdom."

8. Summarize what you have learnt so far about how one gets wisdom:

- for humanity in general

- for an Israelite in the time of Proverbs

But what about us? How do we gain wisdom? We are better off than humanity in general, for we have at least been exposed to the revelation of God in Proverbs. But we are not Old Testament Jews, saved by YHWH, and living in the Promised Land. How are we to read and apply Proverbs rightly today?

A fuller answer will come in study 6, when we see how Proverbs relates to the New Testament and to life this side of Christ. But at this point, we can say wisdom must not only begin with but also continue in the fear of the Lord who saved Israel—for it is this same God that we believe in as Christians today. Just as the Lord was Israel's Father whom they were to fear, so he is our Father whom we fear and trust. Ultimately, the getting of wisdom revolves around not only heeding wisdom's call (see studies 1 and 2), but also relating rightly to the person behind that call. His name is YHWH. He is our Father. It is not merely King Solomon we are to heed, who imparted wisdom as a father to his son, but we are to heed our heavenly Father, the Lord.

» Implications

(Choose one or more of the following to think about further or to discuss in your group.)

- Who or what has been most influential in shaping your decisions about life so far?

- How might this study change where you look for wisdom in this world?

- A 14-year-old boy says to you, "I'm not afraid of my father at all. He can get lost for all I care!" How would you respond to him?

- How have you come to know God better in this study?

- Do you fear God? Why/why not?

- Even if some of the instructions and reproofs in Proverbs seem hard for us to swallow and costly to put into practice, why should we still listen and act?

» Give thanks and pray

- Thank God that he has saved us through his Son, and thus become our heavenly Father. Thank him that we can trust his wisdom on how to live now as his saved people in this world, for this world has been made through his wisdom.
- Pray that we might keep on fearing him, acknowledging, trusting and obeying him in everything, because he is an awesome God who punishes fools and personally disciplines his children.

Endnote

1. B Waltke, *The Book of Proverbs Chapters 1-15*, The New International Commentary on the Old Testament, RK Harrison and Robert L Hubbard, Jr. (gen. eds), Eerdmans, Grand Rapids, 2004, p. 181.

» STUDY 5

DOES PROVERBS PROMISE TOO MUCH?

So far we have seen that the fear of the Lord is the beginning of wisdom, and to act wisely is the stepping stone to a good outcome and success. But is this always the case? Aren't there times when we do wise and right things, and yet it seems to no avail? Does Proverbs promise too much, and need some **counterbalancing**?

Indeed, doesn't the apostle Paul in 2 Timothy 3:12 promise that "all who desire to live a godly life in Christ Jesus will be *persecuted*" (not 'prosperous', as some Christians would have us believe)? Is the writer/collator of Proverbs living on another planet? Doesn't he realize that we live not just in God's creation, but in God's *fallen* creation?

1. What do you think—does the book of Proverbs promise too much? Is it unrealistic?

Counterbalancing

Many argue that Proverbs' wisdom promises too much, and that Ecclesiastes and Job were written to provide some sort of counterbalance within the Old Testament wisdom literature. Ecclesiastes argues that the certainty of death and the injustice of the world make most things in life pretty absurd and frustrating—even wisdom! Job's experience as the righteous man who undergoes severe undeserved suffering seems at odds with Proverbs' simple 'cause and effect' paradigm, where it seems that you just need to 'be wise' and all will go well with you.

Preliminary conclusions

The wisdom of Proverbs, of course, points beyond itself to the New Testament as well. In the next study, we will investigate how the New Testament quotes, alludes to, and applies Proverbs to Jesus and to us. After we have seen Proverbs in the context of the *whole Bible*, we can draw *fuller* conclusions as to whether the wisdom of Proverbs promises too much.

Before we dismiss Proverbs as being too simplistic and in need of correction, perhaps we should look a little closer. In particular, we need to investigate how Proverbs sees itself within God's unfolding plan of salvation in the Old Testament. Does the writer/collator of Proverbs realize that we live in a *fallen* creation? At the end of this study we will draw some **preliminary conclusions** regarding whether Proverbs promises too much.

Proverbs and the Old Testament

2. Look up the following sets of references, and jot down what you notice about how 'wisdom' and 'folly' are reflected in the rest of the Old Testament story.

Proverbs	Compared with	What do you notice?
1:7, 9:10	Exodus 6:1-8	
3:19, 8:22-30	Genesis 1	
8:31	Genesis 1:26-28	
3:7	Genesis 3:4-7	
1:15-16	Genesis 4:8-10, 6:5-6	
1:7, 9:10	Deuteronomy 6:1-9	
28:4-5, 28:7, 29:18	Deuteronomy 4:5-10, 21:18-21	
22:28	Deuteronomy 19:14	
1:1, 8:15, 10:1, 25:1	1 Kings 3:6-14, 4:29-34	
2:20-22	Deuteronomy 28:1-2, 15, 63 2 Kings 17:6-8, 25:1-2	

3. Now see if you can plot the storyline of the Old Testament (as represented by the quotes on page 42) along a time line. Plot the actions above the line if they relate to wisdom, and below the line if they are examples of folly.

Wisdom

Folly

4. Look up the following verses in Proverbs. What do they say about the prosperity of the foolish and the wicked?

- 10:2
- 11:16
- 13:7
- 13:23
- 19:10
- 24:1

- 28:12

- 28:15

- 29:2

- 29:16

5. Look up the following verses in Proverbs. What do they say about prosperity and riches?

- 15:16

- 16:19

- 19:1

- 22:1

- 28:6

6. How then should we respond to wicked, rich fools?

The reign of Solomon represented the height of wisdom in Israel's history. Through Israel's redemption from Egypt, and her entry into the Promised Land, YHWH was fulfilling his promises to Abraham. He was restoring humanity's experience of wisdom that it had forfeited in the folly of the Fall. What other nation had Israel's wisdom, both in the Law of Moses and the reign of Solomon?

As the king of Israel, Solomon in Proverbs addressed his subjects as 'father' to 'son'. Of all people, Solomon's own son Rehoboam should have heeded his wisdom. But after Solomon's death, Rehoboam acted foolishly in increasing the tax burden on his people, and this eventually led to the division of the kingdom (1 Kings 12). Indeed, Solomon himself did not listen to his own wisdom. Instead of fearing the Lord, he turned to the foreign gods of his pagan wives.

After Solomon, both the northern and southern kingdoms of Israel spiralled into sin, foolishness and destruction. The prophets looked forward to another son of David to come, another king of Israel on whom would rest "the Spirit of wisdom and understanding, the Spirit of counsel and might, the Spirit of knowledge and the fear of the Lord" (Isa 11:2). Would there ever be a son of Solomon who would "find favour and good success in the sight of God and man" (Prov 3:4)?

The book of Proverbs is written in the midst of this history, and shows at numerous points that it is well aware of human sin, the injustice of the world, and God's unfolding plan. It seems that the author/collator of Proverbs is not from another planet after all.

» Implications

- When you last worked on the wisdom diagram in study 4 (see page 36), you should have got something like this:

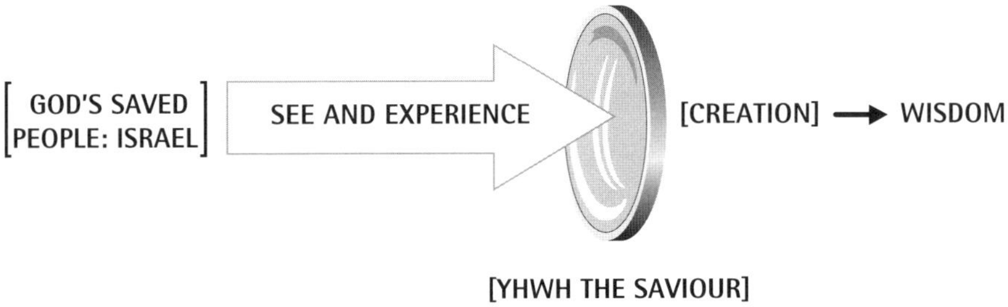

In light of what we've seen in this study, can you make any further improvements?

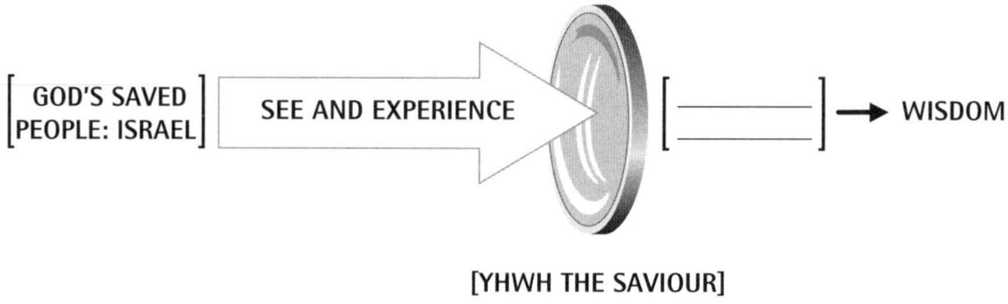

- What attitude should we have to all Old Testament Scriptures, including Proverbs? (Read 2 Timothy 3:14-17.)

- "Does Proverbs promise too much?" We will examine this question further in the next study, but what preliminary observations would you make so far?

» Give thanks and pray

"Keep them and do them, for that will be *your wisdom and your understanding* in the sight of the peoples, who, when they hear all these statutes, will say, 'Surely this great nation is a *wise and understanding* people'." (Deut 4:6)

- Thank God for giving us wisdom to live by—not only in Proverbs, but also as we read Proverbs in the light of the whole Old Testament.
- Pray that we will long for this wisdom, and that this longing will be reflected in our desire to read and apply the Old Testament.

» STUDY 6

WISDOM BEYOND PROVERBS

1. Think back over what you have learned so far about the place of Proverbs in the bigger story of the Old Testament. How would you summarize where Proverbs fits into God's saving history?

2. Do you think Proverbs promises too much? What questions remain unanswered in your mind over this issue?

We've been looking at Proverbs and YHWH's saving history, but of course that history extends beyond the Old Testament. In this study, we will see how Proverbs points beyond itself to the New Testament as well. We will investigate how the New Testament quotes, alludes to, and applies Proverbs to Jesus and to Christians. This will help us further understand whether Proverbs promises too much, and how we should apply its wisdom to our Christian lives.

Proverbs and the New Testament

3. We are used to thinking of the promises and prophecies of the Old Testament being fulfilled in Jesus, but what about the *wisdom* of the Old Testament? Look up the following references and jot down how the wisdom of Proverbs is fulfilled in Jesus.

OT wisdom	Jesus	How is it fulfilled?
Proverbs 1:1	Luke 11:31	
Proverbs 2:3-5	Matthew 13:44 Colossians 2:2-3	
Proverbs 3:4	Luke 2:40, 52	
Proverbs 8:22	Colossians 1:15-16	
Proverbs 10:24-25	Matthew 7:24-27	

As with the rest of the Old Testament Scriptures, Proverbs points forward to Jesus Christ (Luke 24:44-45). He is our Lord and Redeemer. Jesus is the lens through which we now must view Proverbs. And so our wisdom diagram should look like this:

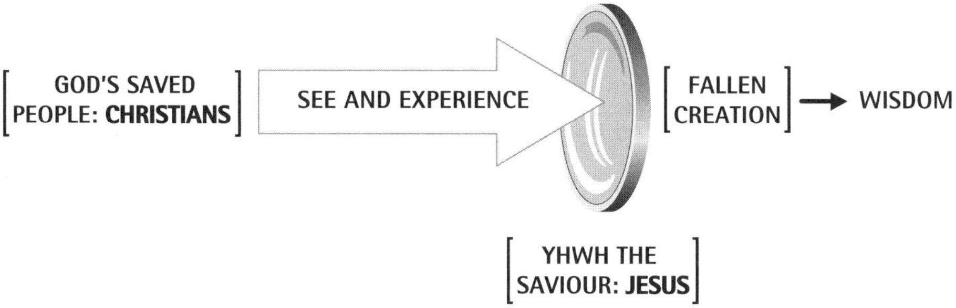

Proverbs is ultimately not written for every man who lives in God's creation, or even just for YHWH's people Israel, who were redeemed by him to live in the Promised Land. In the end, it is written for us who have been redeemed by Jesus. While the proverbial sayings may indeed be useful for anybody living in this creation, Proverbs is especially useful for us who fear not just the creator God, but the Lord who was born as a man, and who died and rose to be lord of all: the Lord Jesus Christ.

The New Testament writers often quote, allude to, and apply parts of Proverbs to the Christian life. From such we can work out a pattern or trajectory of how to apply the rest of Proverbs today.

4. Look up as many of the following verses in Proverbs as you have time for, and quickly jot down how you would apply them to your Christian life. Before you move on to the next verse, look up the corresponding verses to see how the New Testament applies it to us. Lastly, work out whether, according to the New Testament, the consequence promised by the proverb is expected to be experienced *now* in this life, or *not yet*—that is, in the age to come or on judgement day—or *both*. (If you're working in a group, you might like to divide the verses up amongst the group.)

Proverbs	**How would you apply?**	**NT**	**Now**	**Not yet**	**Both**
2:3-6		James 1:5			
3:3-4		Romans 12:17 2 Corinthians 8:21			
3:34		James 4:6,10 1 Peter 5:5			
4:26		Hebrews 12:13			
7:1-3		2 Corinthians 3:3			
10:12		1 Peter 4:8			
11:24		2 Corinthians 9:6			
15:29		James 5:16			

17:3		1 Peter 1:7			
19:17		Matthew 25:40			
19:18		Ephesians 6:4			
20:22, 25:21		Romans 12:19-21			
23:4, 28:22		1 Timothy 6:9			
24:11-12		Matthew 16:27 Revelation 22:12			
24:21		1 Peter 2:17			
26:11		2 Peter 2:22			
27:1		James 4:13-14			
29:23		Luke 14:11			
30:8		Matthew 6:11 1 Timothy 6:8			

5. In light of this exercise, think about the following:

- How would you summarize the way the New Testament applies Proverbs to us today? In what ways is this application distinctively Christian?

- Would you feel confident in applying any saying or passage in Proverbs to us today, even those that are not quoted in the New Testament? How would you go about it?

- How do the last three columns (now, not yet, both) help us in understanding why our present experience does not always match all that Proverbs seems to promise?

"Does Proverbs promise too much?" revisited

By the grace of God, Christians have made a supremely wise choice—to trust and submit to the Lord Jesus Christ. The consequence is eternal *life* instead of eternal *death*—heaven, not hell. It is the wisest decision we will ever make!

Yet eternal life begins now as we live wisely in this creation under Jesus our king. As we read Proverbs through the lens of the New Testament, we know that it is describing the best way to live, even though at times the consequences of our wise actions do not square up to all that Proverbs promises. For while the promises of Proverbs often prove true in this life, there is no 100% guarantee that they always will. We see this in the way that the New Testament uses Proverbs, sometimes casting the promised good consequences of wisdom into the future when Jesus returns. Only then will our wise actions be ultimately vindicated.

In other words, this fallen creation—while marred—is still YHWH's creation. There may be bugs in the system, but it is still a creation hardwired with God's wisdom. Thus our wise actions are often successful here and now. But the bugs are significant enough that only in the new heavens and the new earth will our wise actions be truly seen for what they are.

On the flip side, the bad consequences of folly are often seen now in the destructive effect that foolish behaviour has on individuals and society. However, at times the foolish and wicked seem to succeed in this world, as Proverbs itself recognizes. But on Judgement Day, folly will be fully revealed for what it is.

Moreover, in both Proverbs and the New Testament, the goodness of wisdom lies not only in the success that it brings, but also in the good character that it produces. Acting wisely is inherently good in and of itself. Thus Titus 2 describes the godliness of life that flows from the gospel as being 'sound' or 'healthy' (Titus 2:1). The apostle Paul here is simply echoing the sentiment of Proverbs 3:7-8:

> Be not wise in your own eyes;
> fear the LORD, and turn away from evil.
> It will be healing to your flesh
> and refreshment to your bones.

Correspondingly, the malaise of folly is seen not only in the destruction that it brings, but also in the very sin and ungodliness that flow from man's darkened foolish heart (Rom 1:18-32). Part of God's judgement lies in giving people over to sin and folly itself. Even if the destructive consequences of folly may not yet have had a chance to run their course, they are blatantly foolish for those with eyes to see. At Jesus' return, the foolishness of folly will be evident and unmistakable to all.

At Jesus' return, not only will wisdom and folly be unmistakable, but we will experience the full consequences of wisdom in heaven, or the full consequences of folly in hell. Perhaps we should say that Proverbs did not promise too much; *it did not promise enough.*

» Implications

- "The youngest Christian is wiser than Confucius, Einstein and Gandhi put together." Do you agree? Why/why not?

- "Our world's analysis of what is wise or foolish is often flawed because of the short-term criteria that are used." Do you agree? Explain why/why not.

- A Christian friend says to you, "I don't know what to believe anymore ... I prayed and committed my plans to God, and sought to be obedient, but everything has just turned sour and bad." Using what you have learned in this study, what would you say to your friend?

- Another Christian friend says to you, "I wish I could do what non-Christians do. They seem to be enjoying themselves and I'm missing out!" How would you respond?

» Give thanks and pray

- Thank God that in Jesus and the New Testament you have a greater revelation and wisdom than even Solomon had! In that light, pray that you might rightly respond to Proverbs, as you apply its wisdom through the lens of Jesus.
- Pray about the times when you (or fellow Christians you know) do what's wise and right, and yet it seems to no avail. Pray for courage to persevere in the light of this study.

» STUDY 7

HOW TO GET WISDOM

The beginning of wisdom is this:
Get wisdom,
and whatever you get, get insight.
(Prov 4:7)

For the Lord gives wisdom;
from his mouth come knowledge
and understanding.
(Prov 2:6)

How do we rightly understand and apply the plethora of wise sayings in Proverbs? We know it's our responsibility to *get* wisdom, and we want to make it a priority, but how do we go about it? We know it ultimately depends on the Lord who *gives* wisdom, but how do we rightly hear his words of wisdom?

As we have seen, the key is "the fear of the Lord". Armed with this attitude, and guided by the framework of Proverbs 1-9, let's turn now to all the individual sayings of Proverbs 10-31. How do we make sense of them in all their variety? And how do we apply them to our lives?

Understanding individual sayings

Let the wise hear and increase in
learning,
and the one who understands
obtain guidance,
to understand a proverb and a saying,
the words of the wise and their
riddles. (Prov 1:5-6)

If we read in one sitting any of the chapters of Proverbs 10-31 (as we might with a Gospel or one of the letters of the New Testament), we soon discover that it is far too much to take in. There is no apparent line of thought. The topic keeps changing every few verses, if not every verse! It becomes a bit of a jumble in our brains.

Indeed, the very opening verses of Proverbs tell us that these individual sayings are riddles and parables. Usually each saying has two short juxtaposed clauses, without further explanation. Their very brevity makes them thought provoking. They force us to pause, to ponder, to think harder. How do the two clauses relate to one another? What does the whole saying mean, and how does it relates to our lives?

Let's start by looking at some of the proverbial sayings individually.

1. Here is a scattering of sayings. Take each one and discuss what you think it means.

- A rich man's wealth is his strong city;
  the poverty of the poor is their ruin. (Prov 10:15)

- Better is a dinner of herbs where love is
  than a fattened ox and hatred with it. (Prov 15:17)

- Let a man meet a she-bear robbed of her cubs
  rather than a fool in his folly. (Prov 17:12)

- House and wealth are inherited from fathers,
  but a prudent wife is from the LORD. (Prov 19:14)

- The sluggard buries his hand in the dish
  and will not even bring it back to his mouth. (Prov 19:24)

- Whoever sings songs to a heavy heart
  is like one who takes off a garment on a cold day,
  and like vinegar on soda. (Prov 25:20)

2. Now think back over these sayings, and see if you can work out *how* you worked out what each one meant. What was it about the saying that drove you to your conclusion? Was it the imagery used, comparisons or contrasts, exaggerations, understatements, word repetition, or ...?

3. None of the sayings we've looked at contains direct commands, yet they still motivate us towards certain courses of action. In each of the sayings above, what would be the appropriate course of action?

Not only does one saying after another fail to present a coherent, logical argument (like, say, the letters of Paul do), but the individual sayings themselves are not even cast as commands to be obeyed. Yet despite not having any commands attached to them, they nevertheless spur us to action by making sharp observations about the nature of things. Proverbs describes the way our world *is*, and it describes the consequences that flow from wisdom or folly. In this way, it drives us to action—to what we *ought* to do.

However, moving from the *is* of Proverbs to the *ought* of how we should apply that wisdom is not always simple. Let's investigate further.

4. Take a look at the following proverbs that make sharp observations about the world. How would you apply their wisdom? What do you think these proverbs are calling on us to do?

- A rich man's wealth is his strong city;
    the poverty of the poor is their ruin. (Prov 10:15)

- A bribe is like a magic stone in the eyes of the one who gives it;
    wherever he turns he prospers. (Prov 17:8)

- Wealth brings many new friends,
    but a poor man is deserted by his friend. (Prov 19:4)

- Answer not a fool according to his folly,
    lest you be like him yourself. (Prov 26:4)

5. Now look up the following proverbs that relate to the same subjects. Do they help you to apply the proverbs above? If so, how?

- Proverbs 11:28 (riches)

- Proverbs 16:8, 17:23 (bribery)

- Proverbs 18:24 (friends)

- Proverbs 26:5 (answering a fool)

"Context is your best friend" is a proverb taught to me by one of my Bible teachers. For me to protest, "But my wife is my best friend!" would be to take that proverb out of context! No individual proverb is universal or absolute. To expect a proverb to say everything, even about a particular situation, is to expect too much. Each proverb can make a true observation about a matter without claiming to be the totality of wisdom on that matter. Thus, it is true that bribery brings prosperity (Prov 17:8), but it is also true that dishonest money is just not worth it (Prov 16:8, 17:23).

Moreover, the situations we face day by day, and hour by hour, vary considerably—even if they have superficial similarities. Sometimes it is wise to "look before you leap". But in another situation, "he who hesitates is lost".

Likewise, how should you answer a fool? It depends. If you are in danger of being dragged down to his level, "answer not a fool according to his folly, lest you be like him yourself" (Prov 26:4). But if you can take up his foolish arguments and demonstrate their stupidity for his own good, then by all means "answer a fool according to his folly, lest he be wise in his own eyes" (Prov 26:5).

Indeed, the very succinctness of each individual proverb makes it paramount that we read each one in light of the others. While there are many examples of pairings and groupings of proverbial sayings (e.g. Prov 17:27-28, 18:10-12, 27:5-6), and even whole poems (e.g. 23:29-35 on wine; 31:1-9 on rulers and wine), most individual sayings stand alone in their immediate context.

According to its own introduction, one purpose of this whole collection designated "The proverbs of Solomon" is "to understand a proverb and a saying ..." (Prov 1:1, 6). In other words, the wisdom we gain from whole book of Proverbs ought to help us understand and apply any particular proverb within it. No single proverb ultimately stands on its own, but is to be read and applied in the light of the whole book. In fact, it is very possible to be foolish in using a proverb: "Like a thorn that goes up into the hand of a drunkard is a proverb in the mouth of fools" (Prov 26:9).

Here then is why every talk series or Bible study guide on Proverbs inevitably resorts to dealing with Proverbs 10-31 topically. It is not only for the sake of scratching where people itch (we all love application), nor just for the sake of brevity or avoiding boredom (imagine a 22-week sermon series going through Proverbs 10-31 chapter by chapter), but because it is important for us to see what Proverbs as a whole has to say about a topic. It sets before us in one sitting all the various facets of wisdom on a particular theme. It safeguards us from misapplying any single saying. It gives us perspective and balance on how to live wisely in that area of life. (Our study guide is no exception— the forthcoming volume 2 on Proverbs will deal with these chapters of Proverbs thematically rather than chapter by chapter.)

But then we can't help wondering: Why didn't God arrange the final collection of Proverbs topically?

Reading Proverbs 'as is'

If God intended the collection of sayings to be presented as they are in Proverbs 10-31, it must be for a reason. What is to be gained by reading Proverbs 10-31 'as is'?

6. Read through Proverbs 10-11 (or any other two consecutive chapters in Proverbs 10-31), and then answer the questions below.

- Does the arrangement of sayings seem haphazard?

- What do you think would be *lost* if it was all arranged topically?

- If there is no grouping under particular areas of life (e.g. work, marriage, speech, friendship, etc.), can you see any significant repeated catchwords or phrases as you read through these two chapters?

7. Why do you think God arranged Proverbs 10-31 the way it is? What might he be saying to us about life and wisdom?

If Proverbs sometimes seems like a jumble of topics, it's not hard to see that this is exactly what life is like much of the time. Our lives are not compartmentalized into orderly themes, and neither is Proverbs. Wisdom in one area of life is related to wisdom in another area of life. I can't just say that I'll be wise in my marriage but not in my work or friendships.

Life under God is interconnected. God is not interested in us searching through Proverbs 10-31 to find wisdom on only one particular topic. He wants us to be wise not just in one area, or even a few areas, but in *all* of life. "In all your ways acknowledge him, and he will make straight your paths" (Prov 3:6). He wants us to discover how his wisdom should inform all of life, with all its varied daily challenges and problems.

What's more, God desires us not only to *act* wisely in all of life, but also to *be* wise people. He wants us to be upright, righteous and humble people, rather than wicked, evil and proud. The echo of such phrases is never far away as we read one saying after another in Proverbs 10-31, for such is the character of the wise person (as Proverbs 1-9 has already told us). Thus the mosaic of sayings in Proverbs 10-31 artistically reinforces the introduction that frames it, and vice versa.

Yes, it is useful to gather all the sayings about an area of life into one place, so we can see all the nuances and counterbalances in context (and we'll do that in volume 2 of these studies). Nevertheless, we must keep 'getting' (listening to and understanding) the wisdom of Proverbs 10-31 in the way that Proverbs presents itself, saying after saying, chapter after chapter.

Why not resolve to do that in the weeks to come?

» Implications

- A young Christian says to you, "I don't have the time or the patience to plough through all these verses! Can you just give me a few quick proverbs that will get me through life?" What would you say to him?

- If your life was like a house, are there certain rooms that have a 'Keep Out' sign on the door, where not even God is allowed in?

- Share how wisdom (or foolishness) in one area of your life has spilled over to other areas of your life.

» Give thanks and pray

- Thank God for giving us Proverbs 10-31 as a whole (as well as each individual saying) so that we may be challenged to live all of life in wisdom to please him.
- As you read Proverbs 10-31 in the coming days (and years!), pray that you will always have the attitude of fearing the Lord, for that is "the beginning of wisdom".